PAPERBACK **PLUS**

Contents

No one would ever accuse Paul Robert Walker of having limited interests. He's written books on such diverse subjects as the great baseball player Roberto Clemente; Wild West figures like Sitting Bull, Jesse James, Geronimo, and Wyatt Earp; American tall tales; and even legendary creatures like Bigfoot.

One of his favorite activities, says Walker, is reading his stories out loud to young people — for in doing this, he can combine his love of acting, teaching, and writing into one (as Davy Crockett would say) "totalaciously splendiferous" experience!

"Run for your lives! The dam is breaking!"

On May 31, 1889, an old dam crumbled in the hills above Johnstown, Pennsylvania. A wall of water as high as a seven-floor building exploded into the valley below.

By the time the wave hit Johnstown, it was a muddy stew of trees and buildings, livestock, railroad cars, and hundreds of victims. It struck with such force that it tore the clothes off people's backs. Thousands of men, women, and children fought to survive the flood and the days and nights of horror that followed.

Here is the incredible hour-by-hour account of one of the worst natural disasters in American history—why it happened and how it could have been prevented. It's a story so amazing you've got to **Read It to Believe It**!

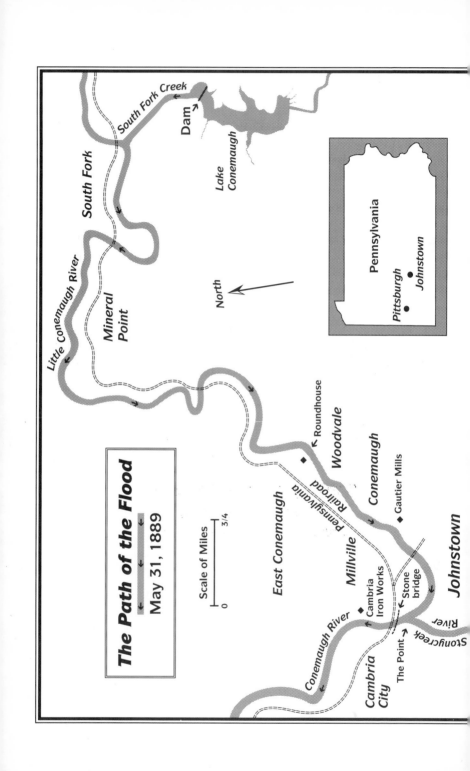

The Path of the Flood
May 31, 1889

South Fork Creek

Dam

Lake Conemaugh

South Fork

Little Conemaugh River

Mineral Point

North

Pennsylvania

Pittsburgh

Johnstown

Roundhouse

Woodvale

Conemaugh

Gautier Mills

East Conemaugh

Pennsylvania Railroad

Millville

Cambria Iron Works

Stone bridge

The Point

Johnstown

Stonycreek River

Conemaugh River

Cambria City

Scale of Miles

0   3/4

Head for the Hills!

The amazing true story of the Johnstown flood

By Paul Robert Walker
With illustrations by Gonzalez Vicente
and photos

TARKINGTON SCHOOL LIBRARY
3414 Hepler Road
South Bend, Indiana 46635

HOUGHTON MIFFLIN COMPANY
BOSTON
ATLANTA   DALLAS   GENEVA, ILLINOIS   PALO ALTO   PRINCETON

Acknowledgments

For each of the selections listed below, grateful acknowledgment is made for permission to excerpt and/or reprint original or copyrighted materials, as follows:

Selections

Head for the Hills! The Amazing True Story of the Johnstown Flood, by Paul Robert Walker, illustrated by Gonzalez Vicente. Text copyright © 1993 by Paul Robert Walker. Text illustrations copyright © 1993 by Random House, Inc. Reprinted by permission of Random House, Inc.

"Make an Embankment Dam," from *How We Build Dams*, by Neil Ardley. Copyright © 1990 by Garrett Educational Corporation. Reprinted by permission.

"Teton: Eyewitness to Disaster," from June 21, 1976, *Time* magazine. Copyright © 1976 by Time, Inc. Reprinted by permission.

Illustrations

104–106, 108–109 Chris Costello

Photography

ii Courtesy of Paul Robert Walker. **97** Banta Digital Group. **98, 100, 101** Dale Howard/Time Inc. **102–103** UPI/The Bettmann Archive. **104** Banta Digital Group.

Houghton Mifflin Edition, 1996
Copyright © 1996 by Houghton Mifflin Company. All rights reserved.

No part of this work may be reproduced or transmitted in any form or by any means, electronic or mechanical, including photocopying and recording, or by any information storage or retrieval system without the prior written permission of the copyright owner unless such copying is expressly permitted by federal copyright law. With the exception of nonprofit transcription in Braille, Houghton Mifflin is not authorized to grant permission for further uses of this work. Permission must be obtained from the individual copyright owner as identified herein. Address requests for permission to make copies of Houghton Mifflin material to School Permissions, Houghton Mifflin Company, 222 Berkeley Street, Boston, MA 02116.

Printed in the U.S.A.

ISBN: 0-395-73256-5

456789-B-99 98 97 96 95

Contents

Chapter 1

The Day Before Disaster

The streets of Johnstown buzzed with excitement. It was Memorial Day, 1889. A day of picnics and a big parade. And this year's parade looked like it might be the biggest ever.

Thousands of visitors poured in from nearby towns. They came by train and horse-drawn trolley, in wagons and carriages, on foot and horseback.

In the park near the center of town, farmers and townspeople spread their picnic lunches on gaily colored blankets. Children chased each other around the big fountain, where six iron swans spit water high into the air.

Cows wandered freely, eating their own picnic from the long green grass. A week earlier the town council had passed a law forbidding cows in the park because they made a mess. But it was not yet official. So the cows enjoyed the holiday too.

Johnstown was the largest city in the Conemaugh Valley, an iron-and-steel center in western Pennsylvania. Its bustling streets were crowded between the Little Conemaugh and Stonycreek rivers.

Most of the men in the valley worked for the Cambria Iron Company. The Cambria mills ran twenty-four hours a day, making steel tracks for the great railroads that criss-crossed America. Other Cambria factories made everything from barbed wire and bricks to wool and flour.

But on Memorial Day, no one was thinking about work.

At the park the picnickers finished their

lunches and joined the huge crowd on Main Street. People had been gathering there all morning, waiting for the parade to start.

Down at the Point, where the rivers met and formed the Conemaugh River, the marchers got ready to step off. The musicians tuned their instruments. The carriage drivers brushed their horses one last time.

A few people noticed that the yellowish-brown water was higher than usual around the Point. But they were not surprised.

It had been a wet spring—the wettest in Johnstown's history. Over 50 inches of rain had already fallen that year. The fields and mountains were oozing with water. All the rivers in the area were rising.

And the dull gray sky promised more rain before the end of the day.

The people of Johnstown were used to rain, and they knew that a downpour would flood the streets. It happened almost every spring.

The water never rose more than a few feet. No one ever drowned. But there was always lots of work to be done: moving carpets, furniture, and important papers to the upper floors until the water went down again.

Yes, there might be flooding tomorrow. But Johnstowners were having too much fun to worry about it. The parade was about to begin!

The mayor led the parade from the Point down Main Street. He wore his best black coat

and top hat and carried a gold-headed cane.

Policemen marched behind him, their polished badges gleaming in the afternoon light. Then came a brass band in scarlet uniforms with golden braid.

More bands followed, from the smaller towns of the valley. A shiny fire engine rolled by, pulled by white horses with red ribbons tied to their harnesses.

Veterans of the Civil War marched next,

wearing the faded blue uniforms of the Union Army.

The cheering crowd grew quiet as they passed. The Civil War had ended in 1865, just 24 years earlier. In 1868 Memorial Day had been established to honor those who died in the war.

The people watching the parade were the brothers and sisters, children and grandchildren, of the dead soldiers of Johnstown.

When the last carriage had rolled by, the crowd stepped into the street and followed the parade. The long line of marchers headed out to Sandy Vale Cemetery. There they placed bright flowers on the graves of the soldiers and said a silent prayer.

When the ceremony ended, the paraders marched back to the center of town and crowded into the Opera House to hear a speech. In the days before television and movies, speeches were a popular form of entertainment.

Outside, the rain began to fall again. The

crowd in the Opera House could hear its gentle patter on the roof.

On the stage the speaker said, "Peace has its dangers and battles as well as war."

The audience had no idea how true those words would prove to be. Within hours they would face the greatest danger of their lives.

By the end of the next day the Opera House would be in ruins a mile away. Main Street and the park would be a mass of oozing mud. The Point would be a fiery nightmare. And over two thousand people in the Conemaugh Valley would be dead.

Chapter 2

The Water Rises

In the mountains above the crowded streets of Johnstown, a disaster waited to happen. It was called the South Fork Dam.

Before the Civil War, Pennsylvania had a system of canals so that goods could be carried by boat across the state. One canal ended at Johnstown.

The dam was built to hold back one of the mountain creeks and form a lake. The lake would provide water for the Johnstown canal during the dry season.

The men who built the dam were experts called engineers. They used only rocks and mud, but they built a strong, safe dam.

When it was finished in 1852, the South Fork Dam was the largest earthen dam in the world: 931 feet long and 72 feet high. That's longer than three football fields and higher than a seven-floor building.

Two years later the Pennsylvania Railroad completed its tracks across the state. Now trains could carry the goods. The canal system was no longer needed, and the dam slowly fell apart.

In the summer of 1862 the dam broke half-way down the wall. Water poured down to the Little Conemaugh River and into Johnstown.

Fortunately, the break happened during the dry season, when the lake and the rivers were low. There was little damage. Many people in Johnstown didn't even know that the dam had broken.

In 1879 a group of rich men from Pittsburgh bought the dam and the land around it. They formed the South Fork Fishing and Hunting Club and began building a summer resort. They repaired the dam to create a lake for fishing and boating.

Some of the richest men in the world belonged to the club. But they did not hire an engineer to fix the dam.

Instead, they had workmen dump rocks and gravel into the broken part of the dam. Then the men filled in the spaces with dirt and hay and spruce branches.

Twice the repairs were washed away by heavy rains. But finally the dam held, and the water began to rise. The club members named it Lake Conemaugh.

In the spring, when the rains filled the mountain streams, the lake was two miles long, a third of a mile wide, and almost 70 feet deep. It contained 20 million tons of water.

The members built beautiful summer homes and a big clubhouse with 47 bedrooms. They hunted in the woods and fished in the clear water of Lake Conemaugh. They sailed their boats and canoes across its smooth surface.

Fourteen miles down the valley, the people of Johnstown lived in a world of hard work and black smoke from the steel mills.

They didn't know much about life on the lake. And most of them didn't worry much about the dam.

In fact, the dam became a joke among the townspeople, especially during a rainstorm. "Head for the hills!" they'd say with a laugh. "The dam is breaking!"

Early on the morning of Friday, May 31, 1889—the day after the parade—Colonel Elias Unger woke up and looked out his window at Lake Conemaugh.

As president of the Fishing and Hunting Club, Unger was the only member who lived at the lake year-round. He owned a farm right next to the dam.

Unger knew the lake and the dam well. And

what he saw that morning filled him with fear.

Rain had been pouring down all night. Water from the surrounding hills and streams was flooding into Lake Conemaugh. It was higher than Unger had ever seen it before.

Unger ran through the driving rain and crossed a wooden bridge that led to the top of the dam. He knelt down and checked the water level.

Yesterday the water had been at its normal level, around six feet below the top of the dam. Now it was only four feet—and rising fast.

Unger looked back at the bridge. Below it was a channel where water rushed around the dam and down into South Fork Creek.

This channel, called a spillway, was the only way to lower the water in the lake. But it was also a way for fish to escape from the lake.

The club members loved fishing, and they spent hundreds of dollars to fill the lake with fish. To keep them in, big iron screens had been built across the spillway. But branches and leaves had been catching in the screens for years, slowly stopping the flow of water.

Unger knew he should remove the screens. But he was afraid to lose the valuable fish. The other club members would be angry.

At the clubhouse, a mile away from the dam, another man also watched the water rising in the lake. But he worried about more than the fish.

John Parke was a young engineer who had been hired to build a new sewer system so the club members could have indoor plumbing. In those days many people had outside bathrooms called outhouses.

Parke was also in charge of the dam. When he saw the rising water, he and a workman jumped into a boat and rowed to the upper end of the lake. Parke wanted to check the streams flowing into Lake Conemaugh.

The men stared in amazement at the water rushing down from the hills. Small streams

had turned into raging rivers that ripped the branches from trees. New streams had appeared on fields and hillsides. Parke later said, "The woods were boiling full of water."

In the lower part of Johnstown, near the Point, people woke up to find water flowing down the streets and into their basements. Horace Rose, a lawyer who lived on Main Street, noticed that the

water was already ruining his new wallpaper.

At 7:00 A.M., when workers arrived for the day shift at the Cambria Iron Company, they were sent back home to help their families. Other businesses soon did the same. Schools closed, and children rushed out to play in the flooded streets.

Around ten o'clock the Little Conemaugh and the Stonycreek poured over their banks, and the muddy river water rushed through the streets of Johnstown. Now the entire town was covered with water from the storm.

At the park the water rose to three feet. Near the Point it was almost ten feet. Men and boys floated back and forth in boats and homemade rafts, helping people move to higher ground.

That morning a wagon driver named Joseph Ross drowned while trying to move a family to safety. Ross, the father of four children, was the first person ever to die in a Johnstown flood.

He wouldn't be the last.

Chapter 3

"*Prepare for the Worst*"

When John Parke returned to the clubhouse, he saddled his horse and rode to the dam.

The young engineer found Colonel Unger directing a group of workmen in the pouring rain. They were building a dirt wall across the top of the dam.

Parke rode back and forth, shouting orders at the workmen. But it was no use. The water in the lake was rising an inch every five minutes.

The top of the dam was packed down hard. Even with a horse and plow, the men could raise the wall only a foot.

Colonel Unger had no choice. He ordered the men to remove the fish screens. But it was too late. The screens were so clogged with branches that the workmen couldn't budge them.

Around 11:00 A.M. the water of Lake Conemaugh began to flow over the center of the dam.

On the other side of the giant wall, water was leaking through the front of the dam into the valley below.

It looked bad. Unger decided that the people in the valley had to be warned.

John Parke jumped on his horse and galloped

down the muddy road to the town of South Fork, two miles below the dam. He found a group of people gathered outside a store, watching the rain pour down.

Parke pulled his horse to a stop. "There's water running over the dam!" he shouted. "It might break at any time!"

Some of the people smiled at each other and then at the boyish-looking engineer. They had heard this kind of talk before. But others took his warning seriously. They ran home to move their families to higher ground.

Parke sent two men across the street to the telegraph tower of the Pennsylvania Railroad. The railroad used the telegraph wires to send messages up and down the tracks.

In those days there were no radios, and the telephone was a brand-new invention. Bigger cities like Johnstown had telephones. But the only way to send a message from South Fork was by telegraph.

The telegraph operator was a young woman named Emma Ehrenfeld. She didn't know if she should believe the warning. People were always making jokes about the dam. But just in case, she telegraphed to the next station down the line, at the village of Mineral Point.

W. H. Pickerell, the operator at Mineral Point, had been working on the Little Conemaugh River for fifteen years. In all that time he had never seen such a terrible storm.

Pickerell and Emma Ehrenfeld signaled back and forth in Morse code, the language used by telegraph operators. Finally, Pickerell decided they should send a message to Johnstown, just to be safe.

No one knows exactly what the message said, but it was probably something like this: SOUTH FORK DAM IS LIABLE TO BREAK; NOTIFY PEOPLE OF JOHNSTOWN TO PREPARE FOR THE WORST.

Frank Deckert, who worked at the Johnstown railroad station, glanced quickly at the message when it reached his desk. He mentioned it to a couple of other men in the office, and they all had a good laugh. That same old nonsense about the dam!

Farther up the narrow valley, John Parke didn't know that people were laughing in Johnstown. He believed he had done his duty. So he rode back up the hill.

By now the water was rushing over the top of the dam. Parke guided his horse carefully through the running water.

The leaks in the front wall were worse, but so far the dam was holding. Maybe it wouldn't break after all.

John Parke rode to the clubhouse to eat his lunch. There was nothing more he could do.

Fourteen miles away, George Swank, editor of the Johnstown *Tribune,* sat in his second-floor office. He was writing about the flood for tomorrow's paper. All morning, people had been calling with unusual stories about the rising water.

One caller had seen a dead horse floating down the Stonycreek. Another reported an overturned boat on Main Street. A man called to say he was standing in his living room in waist-deep water.

At 3:15 P.M. the *Tribune* received a different kind of call. It was Hettie Ogle, operator of the telephone office. Frank Deckert had just called her from the railroad station. The dam was getting worse, he said, and might break at any time.

This was the third message Deckert had received in the last three hours. But it was the first one he took seriously.

From his second-floor window, George Swank looked out over Johnstown. Some of the streets were already under ten feet of water from the rainstorm.

Swank worried about the people of Johns-

Tarkington School Library

town. Dozens had left their homes for the nearby hills. But those who thought they'd be safe on the upper floors of their houses were now trapped. They had nowhere to go. No way to escape.

What would happen if the dam really did burst, Swank wondered, and Lake Conemaugh poured down into the already flooded valley?

It was too horrible to think about.

Chapter 4

The Dam Moves Away

John Parke gulped down his lunch and hurried back to the dam. What he saw filled him with fear—not for himself but for the people of the valley.

The water rushing across the top of the dam had gouged a V-shaped cut in the outer wall. The cut was ten feet wide and four feet deep—and getting bigger every second.

Farther down the front of the dam, huge boulders had tumbled away and leaks spouted everywhere.

As a trained engineer, Parke had to face the

Before the dam broke…

truth. The question was not *if* the dam would break. The question was *when*.

For two hours Parke and Unger watched as more boulders tumbled away and the cut grew bigger, working its way backward through the dam.

Dozens of people had gathered beside them on the rainy hillside—workmen and club members, local farmers and people from South Fork.

They watched in silent horror, thinking of the people below.

Around 3:00 P.M. the final destruction began.

The cut broke through the inner wall, where the lake water pressed against the dam. Then the water poured out through the cut, making it wider and deeper every second.

Finally, at 3:10, there was a roar like thunder and half the dam fell into the valley below.

John Parke later said that the South Fork Dam didn't break, "It simply moved away."

In less than 45 minutes, the entire contents of

...and after.

Lake Conemaugh—all 20 million tons—flowed through the opening in the dam and headed down the valley.

Directly below were the farms of George Fisher and George Lamb. Both men had been warned about the danger earlier that day.

George Fisher moved his wagon, his cow, and his plow to higher ground. When he finished, it was almost three, and he went back to get his wife and children. They were running up a hill just as the wave thundered past and washed away their house.

Farther down the valley, George Lamb and his family also ran to higher ground seconds before the wave hit.

Lamb watched his house climb the 60-foot wall of water and roll around with George Fisher's house. Then both houses smashed into splinters against the rocky hillside.

The flood roared down to the town of South Fork. The valley grew wider here, and the wave spread out until it was about 40 feet high.

In the South Fork telegraph tower, a train engineer named H. M. Bennett sat talking to Emma Ehrenfeld, the operator who had sent John Parke's warning just a few hours earlier.

Suddenly Bennett glanced out the window. People were screaming and running down the streets. Then he saw it—a wall of water roaring down the valley.

Bennett leaped from his chair. His freight train was sitting across a railroad bridge, on the other side of the river—right in the path of the flood! The brakeman and fireman were sleeping in the engine, and two more men were in the caboose.

Bennett raced down the tower steps and across the bridge. He had no time to pull the entire train to safety. So he cut the engine loose from the rest of the cars and shouted back to the men in the caboose. Then he gunned his engine across the bridge.

A split second later, the water smashed over the tracks. It destroyed the bridge, swallowed the rest of Bennett's train, and pounded into the mountainside.

The men in Bennett's caboose were killed instantly. Over 20 buildings were destroyed in South Fork, including the telegraph tower and a huge woodworking mill.

Luckily, most of the townspeople had gone to higher ground. Some had moved because of the rising river. Others had paid attention to John Parke's warning.

Four people lost their lives, but that was only the beginning. The number of dead would grow higher as the flood rushed along the Little Conemaugh River and down the steep, narrow valley.

Below South Fork the wave squeezed between the mountain walls until it reached its greatest height, 89 feet above the river. There it shattered a huge railroad bridge.

The wave was so fast and powerful that it created a raging wind before it. That wind—and a terrible thundering roar—were the only warning some people had that the flood was coming.

At Mineral Point, W. H. Pickerell was still in his telegraph tower. He heard a roar, looked up the valley, and saw a moving mountain of trees and water.

Pickerell climbed out of his tower window onto a tin ledge. A man floated by on the roof of a house. "Mineral Point is swept away!" he screamed. "My whole family is gone!"

Pickerell scrambled down the stairs and escaped to the hills. Seconds later the wave crushed his tower.

Like the people of South Fork, most of those in Mineral Point had already headed for higher ground. Even so, 16 people died in Mineral Point and half the village was washed away.

Next in the flood path were the towns of East Conemaugh and Franklin. Together they had a population of 1,700.

At East Conemaugh the train yard spread for hundreds of feet along the river. Three passenger trains sat in the yard, waiting for a stretch of damaged track to be repaired.

The passengers had been sitting in the trains for hours. They passed the time talking, reading, and glancing out the windows to keep an eye on the rain-swollen river. Around 3:15 they watched the river wash away a railroad bridge just below the train yard.

The passengers chattered nervously, but the conductors calmed them down. After all, one conductor said, the great Pennsylvania Railroad would never let anything happen to its passengers. Would it?

Chapter 5

"The Lake's Broke!"

On the tracks half a mile upriver from East Conemaugh, John Hess sat at the controls of work train number 1124. Hess and his crew had been riding the tracks all day, repairing the damage from the storm.

John Hess never saw the flood. But he heard it coming with a sound like a hurricane. He saw the trees on the mountain suddenly bent double by the powerful wind. And he knew instantly what had happened.

"The lake's broke!" he shouted.

His men ran for safety up the hillside, but Hess stayed and tied down his whistle so it would keep blowing. Then he raced his train backward into East Conemaugh, leaped out, and ran home to save his family.

The passengers and townspeople were used to the friendly toot-toot of the train whistle. But what they heard now was an endless screaming wail that could mean only one thing: Danger. Terrible danger.

The passengers scrambled out in a panic and raced to the hills. Some made it to safety. Others were not so lucky.

John Ross, a handicapped man from New Jersey, struggled out of the train. A brakeman picked him up and tried to carry him to the hillside.

When the giant wave thundered down, the brakeman dropped John Ross and saved himself. Ross was later found among the dead.

The wave swallowed up the train yard, killing 37 people. Most were aboard one train that was swept away. Strangely enough, the other two trains barely moved down the tracks.

But the rest of the yard was a total wreck. Train station, coal shed, machine shop, telegraph tower—all were destroyed. Miles of steel track were washed away or twisted into strange shapes.

The huge brick roundhouse, where nine

engines were being repaired, was picked up by the wave as easily as a giant would pick up a toy. Along with 23 other engines—some weighing 75 tons each—it was hurled down the valley by the flood.

Twenty-eight people died in the streets of East Conemaugh and Franklin. Hundreds of stores, hotels, and homes were destroyed.

It was bad, but it might have been worse. The whistle of John Hess saved many lives.

A mile below East Conemaugh was Woodvale, the nicest, cleanest town in the valley. Woodvale had been built by the Cambria Iron Company as a special place for its best workers.

Row after row of pretty white houses stood between the river and the railroad tracks. Beautiful trees shaded Maple Avenue, the main street. A horse-drawn trolley ran down the avenue.

Over one thousand people lived in Woodvale. Some had already left for the hills because of the rising water in the river. Most waited in their houses for the water to go down, just as it always did.

Around 3:40 P.M., thirteen men from Woodvale stood on a bridge looking up the valley. One of them was Mr. Evans, the mayor. They had come to check the level of the river.

All day they had heard rumors about the South Fork Dam. But they didn't believe them. After all, people had been talking about the dam for years.

Suddenly the men on the bridge heard the horrible roar of the flood. They didn't wait to see it. They ran back to their houses to try and save their families.

Evans grabbed three of his seven children. His wife carried the two youngest, and the two oldest followed behind. The family ran across the railroad tracks and up the hill.

As he scrambled up the slope, Evans dropped one of his children. A neighbor woman running behind scooped up the child and kept on climbing.

Below them, the flood hit with such fury that it tore the clothes off people's backs. Five minutes later Woodvale had disappeared from the earth.

The once-pleasant streets were an endless sea of mud. There were no trees. No railroad tracks. No pretty white houses.

A single building stood along the river, part of a woolen mill. The trolley shed was gone, along with 68 horses and 30 tons of hay.

Three hundred fourteen people were dead. Of the thirteen men on the bridge, Mayor Evans was the only one who saved his whole family.

Beyond Woodvale was Conemaugh, a town of about four thousand. Many of the men worked for the Gautier Steel Company, a giant factory that made barbed wire.

When the flood hit the factory boilers, a column of scalding steam shot high into the air. Then the entire factory, including countless miles of razor-sharp barbed wire, collapsed into the wave.

But it was no longer really a wave—it was a muddy stew of trees and buildings, livestock, railroad cars, barbed wire, and bodies.

A teenage girl who survived the disaster later said, "I thought it was the end of the world."

And now the flood was heading straight for Johnstown.

Chapter 6

Ten Deadly Minutes

George Heiser owned a general store in a higher part of Johnstown. He lived above the store with his wife, Mathilde, and their 16-year-old son, Victor.

In other Johnstown floods the Heiser store had never been under water. But on the afternoon of Friday, May 31, 1889, George Heiser stood behind his counter in water up to his knees.

Heiser sent Victor to the barn to untie their horses. The barn was on higher ground, so it was not yet flooded. But if the water kept rising, the horses would drown.

Victor waded through the backyard and untied the horses so they could move freely—or swim if they had to. As he walked out the barn door he heard a loud crash and a horrible roar.

Across the yard, Victor's parents appeared in an upstairs window. George Heiser was pointing desperately at the roof of the barn, telling Victor to climb on top.

A few days earlier Victor had made a special trapdoor so he could repair the roof. Now he ran back into the barn, scrambled up through the trapdoor, and stepped onto the red tin roof.

Then he saw it: a dark, rolling wall of houses and freight cars, trees and animals. Before his eyes, the deadly flood crushed his house with his parents still standing at the window.

Now the dark wall moved toward him. Victor knew he would die. How long would it take to get to heaven? he wondered. He checked his pocket watch. It was 4:20 P.M.

The flood hit and lifted the barn right off the ground. Victor struggled to stay on the roof as the building rolled over and over like a barrel.

Straight ahead lay the house of their neighbor, Mrs. Fenn. As the Heiser barn crashed into the Fenn house, Victor jumped and landed on Mrs. Fenn's roof. The house collapsed beneath his feet.

Victor crawled up a piece of the roof and grabbed onto another house that floated by. But he could not get a strong grip. He held on with just the tips of his fingers, knowing he couldn't last much longer.

Finally he slipped and fell through space. Again he was sure he would die.

Thud! Victor landed on another hard surface and looked down in amazement. It was the red tin roof of his own barn!

All around him, Victor's friends and neighbors rode the raging flood, screaming in pain and fear.

Victor saw Mr. Mussante, the fruit dealer, float by with his wife and children on a piece of their floor. The walls and roof were gone, but the family was busy packing their belongings into a trunk. Then they disappeared into the dark, swirling stew.

Victor was hurled into a mass of wreckage between a stone church and a big brick building. A huge freight car loomed high above him, and for a third time he thought he would die.

But just as the freight car was about to crush him, the brick building collapsed and Victor shot out into open water. He was still on the roof of his barn.

Now Victor floated over what used to be the park. The grass and the fountain with its six iron swans were somewhere below him—lost under 30 feet of water.

He saw his neighbor, Mrs. Fenn, trying to stay on top of a tar barrel, the only thing she had to hold on to. She was completely covered with the black gooey stuff. But she kept her head above the flood.

He saw the servant of a local doctor, naked on the roof of the doctor's house. The man was shivering in the cold rain and praying to God for mercy.

The rushing water carried Victor past the Point toward a stone railroad bridge over the Conemaugh River. Beside the bridge a hill rose

more than five hundred feet above the valley.

The floodwater smashed into the hill, and tons of wreckage piled up against the bridge. The hill and the mountain of wreckage slowed the flood and forced the rushing water backward, over the streets of Johnstown and up the Stony-creek.

Victor rode his barn roof across the Stony-creek and into the southern part of Johnstown. There he floated past a group of people huddled together on the roof of a brick building.

It looked like a safe place. So he jumped off his barn roof and onto the brick building, amazed that he was still alive.

Victor Heiser took out his pocket watch and checked the time. It was not quite 4:30.

Johnstown had been completely destroyed in less than ten minutes.

Chapter 7

Thrown Together

Around four o'clock, six-year-old Gertrude Quinn was sitting on the front porch of her big brick house. She dangled her bare feet in the water and watched a family of ducks swimming among the purple flowers in her yard.

Gertrude's father stepped angrily behind her. Unlike most people in Johnstown, he was worried about the dam. When the streets began to flood, he had ordered his children to stay inside the house. He sent Gertrude upstairs to change into dry clothes.

Nervously, Mr. Quinn glanced toward the east, where the Little Conemaugh flowed out of the mountains into Johnstown. Suddenly he heard the rumble of the flood and saw a strange, dark cloud in the sky.

No one knows exactly what produced this cloud. It might have been tiny pieces of wreckage ground up by the flood, or the scalding steam from the Gautier steelworks. Whatever it was, the survivors called it the "death mist."

Mr. Quinn raced inside the house and shouted at his family to run for the nearby hills. He picked up Gertrude's baby sister and splashed out through the flooded streets. Two older sisters rushed behind.

Gertrude followed with her Aunt Abby, her baby cousin, and the baby's nurse. But Aunt Abby refused to step into the cold, muddy water in the street. She thought it would be safer in the house. So they ran upstairs to the third-floor playroom.

Screaming for her father, Gertrude stared out the window at the people scrambling through the watery streets below. "It was like the Day of Judgment," she later wrote. "Animals and humans with eyes bulging out of their heads."

Suddenly the raging flood ripped open the floors and walls of Gertrude's house. Aunt Abby, her baby, and the nurse were sucked down into the yellow water and drowned.

Gertrude grabbed onto the bottom of the roof. A mattress floated up from the second floor. She dropped onto it and rode it like a raft.

A dead horse bumped into her raft and almost flipped it over. Then the horse caught onto a log and floated away, bobbing up and down on the water. Gertrude thought it looked like a strange rocking horse.

Then she saw a group of people riding on a giant roof. Gertrude shouted for help. The people on the roof argued about whether or not they should try to save her.

Suddenly a man with a moustache jumped off the roof and swam through the flood toward the little girl. He was a young steelworker named Maxwell McAchren.

Maxwell pulled himself onto the mattress,

and Gertrude wrapped her arms around his neck. She hung on tight as the raft raced through the floating wreckage, the rain still pounding down around them.

Gertrude and Maxwell passed a hotel that was built on a hillside, above the flood. Two men leaned out the window, shouting for Maxwell to throw Gertrude to them.

"Do you think you can catch her?" Maxwell yelled.

"We can try!" the men replied.

Gertrude shook with fear as Maxwell threw her across 15 feet of water. One of the men in the window caught her!

Gertrude was cold and tired and covered with mud. Most of her clothing had been torn off. But she was safe.

Reverend Chapman lived across from the park, in the heart of Johnstown. All day he had watched anxiously as the water from the storm rose in the streets. By afternoon he noticed with

relief that the level of the water seemed to be going down.

A little before 4:00 P.M., Reverend Chapman glanced out his window. The water was suddenly rising again. He opened the door and saw a freight car floating down the street with a man standing on the roof.

As the freight car floated past the front yard, the man grabbed a tree branch, swung himself up onto the porch roof, and climbed in through the Chapmans' second-floor window.

Reverend Chapman knew immediately that the dam had broken. "Run for the attic!" he shouted.

As his family raced upstairs, Chapman stopped to turn off the gas flame in the fireplace, so it wouldn't set the house on fire. He was about to climb the hall stairs when a huge wave rolled through the front door.

Reverend Chapman ran through the kitchen and made it up the back stairs just in front of the wave.

The Chapman family was joined in the attic by the man from the freight car and two boys who jumped from the roof of a restaurant.

The little group watched in horror as the big brick buildings of Main Street crumbled into the flood. The Chapman house was one of the few buildings left standing.

Suddenly another man washed through the window. He was from the Middle East, and he did not speak much English.

The man kept talking about his father and mother and a trunk with three hundred dollars. He had been saving money to bring his parents to America, and now the money was gone.

The poor man was cold and shivering and afraid. His clothes had been washed away. Reverend Chapman found him some dry clothes and a blanket.

Then they all prayed to survive the night.

In the lower part of town near the Point, Horace Rose leaned out his second-floor window to talk with his neighbors, Mrs. Fronheiser and her daughter Bessie. Ten feet of water from the storm lapped at the walls below.

The houses were only a few feet apart. So Mr. Rose tied a piece of candy to a broomstick and handed it across to Bessie. Then he hung a tin cup of coffee on the broomstick and handed it to Mrs. Fronheiser.

Mrs. Fronheiser was just taking her first sip when they heard a loud crash. "What is it?" she asked.

Rose ran up to the third floor and gazed in horror at the black wall of water, mist, and wreckage destroying the town.

Before he could warn them, Mrs. Fronheiser and Bessie were dead—crushed beneath the crumbling walls of their house.

Horace Rose was crushed too. His face was cut; his ribs, collarbone, and right arm were broken. But he was alive.

Lying in pain, Rose floated on a broken roof

up the Stonycreek. Part of his family, their maid, and two strangers floated with him. Two of his sons had disappeared.

They were out of the raging path of the flood, but they tossed for hours on the waves. The roller skating rink floated past them like a huge ship. Then a soda fountain and a church organ went by.

Later they drifted past the steeple of St. John's Catholic Church, crackling with fire above the water. Flames climbed toward the cross on top, until finally the whole steeple collapsed into the flood.

To Horace Rose and his family, it seemed strange to see a fire in the middle of the water. But it was only one of many fires that night.

Across the flooded town, the worst fire had already begun.

Chapter 8

Floating Bodies and a Fiery Grave

At the stone bridge just beyond the Point, the wave stopped. The horrible wreckage of the flood began to pile up against the bridge. Soon it spread over more than 30 acres.

One man later called it "all the filth of seven towns, all the animals and almost all the men and women that lived in them."

The flood backed up behind the wreckage, forming a new lake over the streets and buildings of Johnstown. In some places it was 30 feet deep.

But the wave could not be stopped for long.

After twenty minutes the water cut a new path around the bridge and right through the side of a hill. The path was 700 feet wide and 25 feet deep.

The water rushed past the bridge and flooded the Cambria steel mills, burying trains and machinery under mud and rocks.

As the water flowed on, it pulled dozens of people along. One of them was Maxwell McAchren, the young steelworker who had tossed Gertrude Quinn to safety.

McAchren rode the mattress past the stone bridge and into the Conemaugh River. He was pulled out at the village of Sang Hollow, four miles past Johnstown.

It was from Sang Hollow that the outside world first learned about the Johnstown flood.

A little after four o'clock, a Pennsylvania Railroad train had stopped there, bound for Johnstown. But the telegraph operator couldn't get through to Johnstown, so he kept the train in

Sang Hollow until he could find out what was wrong.

One passenger was Robert Pitcairn, an official of the railroad. He was also a member of the South Fork Fishing and Hunting Club.

When Pitcairn saw people floating down the river at Sang Hollow, he knew the dam had broken. He rushed a telegram to Pittsburgh with the first news of the disaster.

Another passenger was 17-year-old Bill Heppenstall. Bill watched as a house floated by and caught in some trees hanging over the river. He could hear a baby crying inside the house.

While other passengers discussed what to do, Bill dove into the cold, swirling water. He swam to the house and returned with the baby. Then he swam back and saved the baby's mother.

Most people were not so lucky. By sunset the telegraph operator at Sang Hollow had counted 119 people—dead and alive—floating down the river. Seven were rescued.

*The fire at the bridge, shown in this 1890 painting,
burned for three days and nights.*

As it grew dark, the people at Sang Hollow
noticed a red glow in the sky over Johnstown.
They didn't know it, but the mountain of wreckage at the stone bridge had caught fire.

No one ever found out how the blaze began, but it might have started with a cooking stove. Even though the wreckage was wet, the fire spread quickly. There were plenty of wooden buildings and oil from the railroad cars to feed the flames.

When the fire began, over five hundred people were trapped in the wreckage. Desperately they tried to climb over the jumble of houses and boxcars and barbed wire.

A railroad worker at the bridge said the victims were stuck "like a lot of flies on flypaper, struggling to get away with no hope and no chance to save them."

A 19-year-old girl named Rose Clark was pinned in the wreckage—half in the water and half out. Her arm was broken, and her broken leg was caught on something under the water.

A group of men worked for hours trying to lift her out. But they couldn't move her leg.

As the fire raged closer and closer to Rose,

the men talked about cutting off her leg to save her. Rose asked a priest who was with the workers to give her the blessing for people who are about to die.

At last, one of the men dove down into the water to see what was holding Rose's leg. He found a dead man in the water, his hand wrapped around Rose's ankle. The dead man's muscles were frozen tight.

The rescuers cut off the hand. Then they lifted Rose Clark out of the burning wreckage.

Chapter 9

"Send Coffins"

As night fell, thousands of survivors huddled together in the hills around Johnstown.

They shivered in the cold rain, and their stomachs ached with hunger. They were dazed and frightened and filled with horror.

In the flooded streets of the town, the water was still 20 feet deep. Hundreds were trapped in the upper floors of their houses. They could hear water lapping against the walls below. Sometimes they heard the crash of a nearby building as it collapsed into the flood. They wondered if their own building would be next.

For those near the fire, the sounds were even worse. All night long they listened to the cries and moans of the victims caught in the burning wreckage. But they were trapped themselves, and there was nothing they could do to help.

Two hundred sixty-four survivors made it to the safety of Alma Hall, the largest building still standing. They had no blankets and nothing to eat or drink. Some of the men caught rainwater from the roof in containers and gave it to the children.

Many of those at Alma Hall were injured or in a state of shock. They had no medicine or bandages. One man, Doctor Matthews, did what he could to get them through the night—even though he had two broken ribs himself.

Doctor Matthews helped two women give birth to babies during the night. Another baby was born in the attic of a floating house. Altogether, six babies were born in Johnstown that night. Two were named Flood.

Finally the long, dark night ended. The morning dawned cold and gray. But at least it was light. And the rain had stopped.

Reverend Chapman looked out from his attic

window at what used to be the town park. A lone rooster perched on some wreckage above the water. The rooster flapped its wings and crowed to greet the day.

To Reverend Chapman it seemed as if the rooster was saying, "Cheer up! All is not lost!"

Gradually the water went down, and the survivors made their way into the streets. What they saw was worse than they had imagined.

Railroad cars and heavy machines stuck up out of the mud. Gas lines had broken, and fires burned everywhere. Thousands of bricks were scattered around, washed down from Woodvale, over a mile upstream.

Only a few buildings still stood in their original places. Houses that used to be in Woodvale or Conemaugh were now in Johnstown.

The Opera House lay shattered among the wreckage at the railroad bridge. A four-story brick hotel was totally destroyed. Even the basement would have to be dug again.

The flood had completely swept away an area

two miles long and half a mile wide. One man wrote that "not a stick of timber or one brick on top of another was left to tell the story."

The streets were gone too—lost under the mud. Every tree in the park had been uprooted and washed away. Every fire hydrant had broken off.

The dead were everywhere. Trapped in houses. Buried under wreckage. Stuck deep in the mud. Many bodies were found with their arms stretched upward—as if they were trying to grab on to something. Their noses and ears were clogged with mud.

One elderly lady was found dead, sitting on her rocking chair, at Sandy Vale Cemetery.

Hundreds of dead animals littered the muddy streets and floated in the swollen rivers. Horses, cows, mules, dogs, cats, pigs, goats, chickens, rats. All drowned.

The survivors had little food and no safe water. Many of them climbed into the hills. Some kept walking until they found shelter with farmers in the mountains.

Other survivors tried to help those who were stranded in attics and on rooftops. Still others searched for their families and friends.

Victor Heiser went looking for his parents. He had last seen them in the window of their house when the flood hit.

Victor made his way to the railroad bridge, where the wreckage was burning out of control. There he gave up looking for his parents and went to work helping people at the bridge.

Gertrude Quinn was so dirty and scared that at first no one could recognize her. But early that morning a relative found her and went to get her father.

Mr. Quinn ran to the house where Gertrude was waiting. She jumped into his arms and hugged him tight.

The survivors got busy. They held a meeting and formed groups for different projects.

One group would clean up the wreckage and get rid of the dead animals. Doctor Matthews and another doctor would set up hospitals. Other groups would gather food supplies and keep people away from unsafe buildings. A couple of men cut police badges out of tin cans.

The saddest job of all was given to Reverend Chapman and another minister named Reverend Beale—setting up morgues where the dead bodies would be collected, counted, and prepared for burial.

Churches, schoolhouses—even the men's waiting room at the railroad station—were turned into morgues.

All over the Conemaugh Valley, the gruesome business of burying the dead began. Earlier that morning a lawyer from Cambria City sent a telegram to Pittsburgh.

"Send coffins," he said. "We are without an undertaker. Send coffins of all sizes."

Chapter 10

The World Lends a Hand

The first news of the Johnstown flood was the telegram Robert Pitcairn sent from Sang Hollow. Later that night he sent a longer message, asking for help.

Pitcairn was a powerful man. His requests were taken seriously.

On the day after the flood, a meeting was held in Pittsburgh. People packed the building, eager for news. Pitcairn reported what he had seen floating down the river at Sang Hollow.

In less than an hour the people at the meeting had donated over $48,000 to help the flood victims. (Today this would be worth over $750,000.) Wagons were sent out into Pittsburgh to collect food and supplies.

At 4:30 on Saturday afternoon, exactly twenty-four hours after the flood destroyed Johnstown, the first relief train left Pittsburgh. It was 20 boxcars long.

Doctors, policemen, and reporters rode in one car, along with 75 workmen. Another car held nothing but coffins. The rest of the train carried food, medicine, clothing, and lumber.

At Sang Hollow the train stopped because a section of track had washed out. A work train was making repairs, but it might take hours.

The men from Pittsburgh decided that Johnstown couldn't wait. They unloaded food from two boxcars. Carrying the food on their backs, they crossed the wet, slippery hillside around the damaged section of track.

On the other side the men loaded the food onto two handcars. The work train pulled the handcars up to the stone bridge at Johnstown. It was 1:30 on Sunday morning.

The wreckage piled against the bridge still crackled and smoked, filling the night air with the sickening smell of burning flesh. By the red glow of the fire, relief workers passed out food to survivors huddled on the bridge.

Around eight in the morning the track had been fixed, and the rest of the relief train arrived. Workers built a swinging rope bridge to carry supplies into Millville—located across the new river that the flood had carved into the hillside.

From Millville, the workers crossed the raging Conemaugh River in small boats, bringing supplies into Johnstown.

To the people of Johnstown, the train brought more than food and supplies. It brought hope. The world knew about their terrible disaster. The world would help them.

And the world did help.

Even before the first relief train arrived, a few newspaper reporters had made their way to Johnstown. Within days there were 100 reporters in the town.

The Johnstown flood was the biggest news story since the death of Abraham Lincoln. For two weeks reporters sent out 100,000 words a day over the telegraph wires. The sad tale of death and disaster touched people around the world.

Relief efforts were organized all over the country. Supplies poured in to Johnstown from far and near.

Walla Walla, Washington, more than 2,000 miles away, sent a boxcar full of potatoes. A nearby Pennsylvania town sent 11,000 loaves of bread.

Cincinnati sent 20,000 pounds of ham. Detroit sent 30 dozen chairs. Another shipment included 7,000 pairs of shoes.

While people across the country donated all

they could, the South Fork Fishing and Hunting Club gave little.

South Fork's members were among the richest men in the world. And their dam had caused the disaster. But the club sent only $3,000 and one boxcar full of blankets. Individual club members gave around $20,000 more.

This was a tiny fraction of the $3.75 million donated by the people of the United States and 14 other countries.

The club turned its back on the survivors of the flood. But plenty of others gave a helping hand. Almost 10,000 relief workers went to Johnstown in the days after the disaster.

One of them was Clara Barton, founder of the recently formed American Red Cross. Five days after the flood, she arrived with a team of doctors and nurses.

They set up hospitals in large tents and went through town looking for people who needed medical help. Later the Red Cross built wooden "hotels" to shelter the homeless survivors.

Other relief workers set up supply stations throughout the valley to hand out food and clothing.

There was little meat, milk, or fruit but an

Some survivors made temporary shelters and tried to rebuild their lives. Others left town and never came back.

endless supply of jam and bread. The food wasn't fancy, but no one starved. Clothing donations were so generous that some survivors were better dressed after the flood than they were before.

While relief workers fed and clothed the living, dead bodies and rotting garbage still littered the muddy streets. Twelve days after the flood, the state of Pennsylvania took over the clean-up effort.

State health workers buried the human dead and burned the dead animals and garbage. They spread tons of chemicals on the streets to prevent disease. Years later, survivors remembered the smell of the chemicals and the black flies that swarmed around the garbage.

At the railroad bridge, demolition experts broke up the mountain of wreckage with dynamite. For weeks the explosions shook the town, shattering windows and chimneys and driving people half-crazy.

Four days after the disaster, mill workers

began cleaning up the waist-high layer of mud at the Cambria Iron Company. By the end of June, the mills were back in operation, belching smoke over the valley and turning out steel rails.

The Gautier steelworks did not reopen until August. Men pulled heavy machines and tangled barbed wire out of the mud and hauled them back to where the factory had once stood.

Throughout the Conemaugh Valley, carpenters hammered together new wooden buildings, and bricklayers built new walls. Relief groups bought over 700 ready-made houses for homeless families. New streets and sidewalks were laid.

Gradually life in Johnstown returned to normal. The *Tribune* published a newspaper on June 15. A shipment of watermelons arrived on June 28. An ice cream store opened for the Fourth of July.

Meanwhile, the survivors kept searching for their loved ones.

Sometimes the search ended happily. Horace

Rose found the two sons he lost during the flood—alive. But other survivors were not so fortunate.

Victor Heiser found his mother's body a week after the flood. Days later a man showed Victor another body. He said it was Victor's father. But the body was so damaged that Victor could not be sure.

All that Victor had left was a wooden chest found on a pile of wreckage. Inside were his mother's Bible, some pieces of silverware, and his father's Civil War uniform with one old penny in the pocket.

Victor's neighbor, Mrs. Fenn, lost her husband and all seven of her children. A few weeks after the flood, Mrs. Fenn gave birth to a new baby, but the baby died.

All summer and fall, the dead were removed from the mud and wreckage. The body of Bessie Fronheiser—the little girl who took candy from Horace Rose—was not found until August. Two bodies were found in 1899, ten years after the flood. Another body was found in 1911.

No one knows exactly how many people died in the Johnstown flood. The official number is 2,209. About half of these were killed in Johnstown. The others died in the smaller towns of the valley.

Ninety-nine whole families were wiped out. Ninety-eight children lost both their parents. When the Johnstown schools opened in October, there were 300 fewer students.

About one third of the dead were never actually identified. Their bodies were so damaged that no one could be sure who they were. Some people were missing and never found.

On May 31, 1892, exactly three years after the flood, a crowd of 10,000 people gathered at Grandview Cemetery, on a hillside high above Johnstown.

There they dedicated a stone monument to

the unknown victims of the flood. Behind the monument were over 750 white marble head-stones, neatly arranged on the hillside.

There were no names on the headstones, for the bodies beneath them were never identified. No one would ever know who was buried on that hill.

But the people at Grandview Cemetery did know this: the white headstones stood for their mothers and fathers and children, their husbands and wives, their neighbors and friends.

The blank white stones told the sad story of the Johnstown flood.

After the Flood

The members of the South Fork Fishing and Hunting Club never returned to their 47-bedroom clubhouse or their fancy cottages. The South Fork Dam was never rebuilt. Grass and trees grew where Lake Conemaugh once stood.

Johnstown blamed the club for the disaster. Newspapers around the country agreed.

Several court cases were brought against the South Fork club. But neither the club nor its members were ever found guilty. The disaster taught a painful lesson: that people do not always take responsibility for their actions.

In November 1889, Johnstown and seven nearby towns united to form the new city of

Johnstown. As the mayor they elected Horace Rose, who had recovered from his injuries.

Rose and the city government set out to make Johnstown safe from floods. Workmen dug dirt and rocks out of the rivers and lined some of the river banks with concrete.

Johnstown began to grow again. The steel mills boomed. By 1930, there were 100,000 people in Johnstown and the surrounding area.

In 1936 another big flood hit the town. This time a dam did not break. But the rivers overflowed after two days of rain and flooded the streets. Twenty-five people drowned, and over two thousand buildings were damaged.

Between 1938 and 1943, army engineers worked to make Johnstown safe from floods. They cut the rivers deeper and lined the banks with concrete for nine miles. The project cost over $7,000,000.

Now everyone was sure that Johnstown would never be hit by another big flood.

Then in July 1977, it happened again. Almost 12 inches of rain fell in seven hours. The river rose 34 feet at the Point in just ten hours. Even the big concrete walls built by the army engineers could not control the raging flood.

Eighty people died. When the water went down, the citizens of Johnstown had to face the awful truth.

Johnstown will never be safe from floods.

Johnstown Flood Facts

Most numbers in this book, including the numbers below, are estimates. There are few exact figures for the power and destruction of the flood. Values are in 1889 dollars. One dollar in 1889 would be worth over $16 today.

The Power of the Flood

Water in Lake Conemaugh..........20,000,000 tons

Time it took to empty...................36–45 minutes

Average height of wave.........................20–40 feet

Greatest height of wave...............................89 feet

Average speed of wave ....14 mph

Greatest speed of wave ....40 mph

Wreckage at the stone bridge ....30–60 acres

The Victims

Total number of dead 2,209

Unidentified bodies 755

Whole families killed 99

Children who lost both parents 98

Children who lost one parent.........................470

Husbands who lost wives 198

Wives who lost husbands 124

Homes destroyed...1,600

Businesses destroyed or badly damaged.........280

Businesses not badly damaged 20

Total value of property damage.........$17,000,000

The Relief Effort

Boxcars full of relief supplies 1,408

Total weight of supplies ....17,000,000 pounds

Money given to help survivors $3,742,881.78

Damages collected from
South Fork Fishing and Hunting Club.............$0

Want to Know More?

Books

Angry Water: Floods and Their Control by R.V. Fodor (Dodd, Mead & Company, 1980, 64 pages). A look at how earthquakes, rainstorms, and hurricanes cause floods; how floods can be controlled; and how the National Weather Service works to forecast floods and prevent loss of lives and property.

The Day It Rained Forever: A Story of the Johnstown Flood by Virginia T. Gross (Viking, 1991, 64 pages). A fictional story about a family that lives through the Johnstown flood. It will give you a good idea of what the flood was like.

When you are older, you might want to read

The Johnstown Flood by David G. McCullough (Simon and Schuster, 1968, 302 pages). It is the best adult book about the flood.

Nature Runs Wild by Karen O'Connor Sweeney (Franklin Watts, 1979, 128 pages). True disaster stories, plus tips on how to survive tornadoes, earthquakes, floods, and other catastrophes.

The Story of Clara Barton by Zachary Kent (Childrens Press, 1987, 32 pages). An illustrated biography of the founder of the American Red Cross.

Museums

Johnstown Flood Museum, 304 Washington Street, Johnstown, Pennsylvania, 15901.

Johnstown Flood National Memorial, Lake Road, St. Michael, Pennsylvania, 15951 (at the site of the dam).

Both museums feature exhibits, photographs, and a film about the flood.

Film

The Johnstown Flood, directed by Charles Guggenheim (one hour). A half-hour version of this film was made for the Johnstown Flood Museum. It was expanded when new photographs of the South Fork Club were discovered. It was shown on the PBS series "The American Experience." Watch for reruns or check the video section of your local library.

Index

Teton:
Eyewitness to
DISASTER

photos by Dale Howard

TIME
OUR NEXT PRESIDENT
(PICK ONE)

"**T**his wet spot on the side of the dam started spurting a little water and I asked my mother, 'Do you think we should notify the authorities?' She said, 'I don't think it could be too serious because nobody is sticking his finger in the hole.'"

It was a warm Saturday morning. Dale Howard, 33, on vacation with his wife Linda and three daughters and visiting his parents in Idaho, had stopped around 10:15 at the newly completed Teton Dam, 40 miles northeast of Idaho Falls. Standing on an observation platform overlooking the 3,000-ft-long, 307-ft-high earth-fill dam, Howard, a geography professor at

After vainly trying to fill a break in the embankment of Teton Dam, two "cat" operators back toward safety as their bulldozers slide into the widening gap.

Minot State College in North Dakota, began taking routine tourist pictures with his Yashica 35-mm camera. As he watched, "the hole started growing — quite slowly at first — forming a small waterfall down on one side. It still looked like just a minor leak."

Then, as Howard kept shooting the remarkable pictures on the following three pages, the drama unfolded below him. Around 11 a.m. two "cat" operators, alerted to the trouble, drove their bulldozers down the slope of the dam and began trying to plug the leak by shoving boulders into the growing hole. As Howard recalled to Reporter Susan Snyder: "My wife was excited and my kids were crying because they thought that the world was coming to an end. It was really frightening. If I had had a weak heart, maybe it would have stopped." Now the big cat had stalled, and the smaller one was trying desperately to pull it back from the widening hole. Suddenly, both drivers scrambled to safety just seconds before the cats plunged into the hole, disappearing briefly, and then were shot out into the valley below by the rushing water. "The hole was enormous, and huge chunks were breaking off," says Howard. "By this time you could see daylight through the hole. It was almost like a natural bridge. Then [at 11:57] the whole thing fell, and it was a raging torrent."

As the embank-
ment crumbles, a
torrent of water
rushes into the
valley below,
pushing dust and
mist before it.

When the water hit the power plant below, recalls Howard, "it just disintegrated. The water picked up a huge oil tank like a cork and away it went. There was a beautiful grove of cottonwood trees down below, and they were snapped off like matchsticks. Later I

Interstate 15 in Blackfoot, Idaho, is closed by the flood waters.

could see the water out on the plain. It was almost like a surrealist picture: as the water hit some of the farm fields, you could see an eerie cloud of dust and mist rise up three to five miles away." ■

How We Build
Embankment
Dams

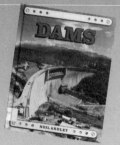

by Neil Ardley

An embankment dam forms a massive barrier across a valley. The front of the dam slopes down to the bottom of the valley, and it is covered with grass or bare rock. Often there is a road along the top of the dam. On the other side of the dam, the water rises almost to the top.

SLOPING SIDES••••••••••••••••••••••••••••

If you could see the whole embankment dam without the water, you would see a wall of soil or rock shaped like an enormous triangle. Both sides of the dam slope outwards from the top. The dam is built in a triangular shape so that it is thickest at its base, where the pressure of water against the dam is greatest.

The side that is under the water is often covered with rocks or stones, which protect the dam. Without this cover, waves would beat against the dam and tear away the soil.

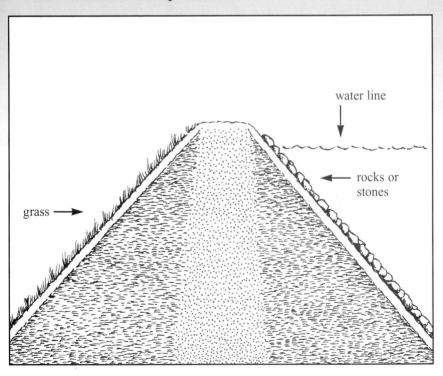

water line

rocks or stones

grass →

An embankment dam is not naturally water-tight. Water can seep through the soil and rock that form the dam. It can also seep through the ground under the dam. Seeping water can weaken the dam and could make it give way.

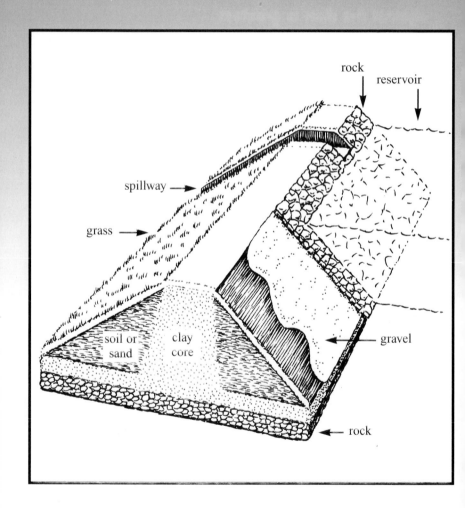

Therefore, embankment dams contain a **core.** The core is a barrier placed inside the dam to stop water from seeping through. Often it is made of clay, which does not absorb water.

Underneath the dam, there may be another barrier, called a **cut-off** or curtain, to stop water from getting through. The cut-off goes down into the ground until it reaches hard rock, so it may be very deep. Usually it is made of clay or concrete.

PREVENTING A FLOOD

Usually, there is a wide channel called a **spill-way** at the side of an embankment dam. If the water in the reservoir becomes too high, water overflows into the spillway and, through it, down into the valley.

The spillway keeps the reservoir at a safe level and prevents the water in the reservoir from flooding over the top of the dam. If that happened, the water would tear away the soil or rock in the dam, and the dam would collapse.

◄ An embankment dam is made of layers of soil or sand around a central clay or rock core. The weight of water on the sloping side helps to keep the dam stable.

Make Your Own Embankment Dam

You will need: a large plastic tray, some soil or sand, water, and a plastic bag

1. Take the tray outside. Lay it on a flat surface. Shape the soil or sand into a firm dam across the middle of the tray.

2. Fill the tray with water on one side of the dam. Watch what happens. How long does it take for the water to leak through the sides and under the dam?

3. Now pour away the water and rebuild the dam. Look at the picture to see how to put the plastic bag in the middle of the dam, so that it acts like a clay core in a real dam.

4. Repeat the experiment. What happens when you pour in the water? How long does it take for the water to leak through the dam this time?